Managing Smart
Technology (MST)

Managing Smart Technology (MST)

Michael D. Wilson

XULON PRESS

Xulon Press Elite
2301 Lucien Way #415
Maitland, FL 32751
407.339.4217
www.xulonpress.com

Printed in the United States of America.

ISBN-13: 978-1-54565-686-0

Introduction

Technology has evolved rapidly in a constant fashion. This is good, but the misnomer of its evolution is that all problems will be solved with technological advancements. To further support this fact is that the multiple components of an **Information Technology Technical System (ITTS),** i.e. processors, database technology, programming languages etc., all evolve at a different pace, never changing simultaneously at the same point in time.

An **ITTS** is the hardware and software infrastructure components that make up a computing system environment.

Figure A. Information Technology Technical System

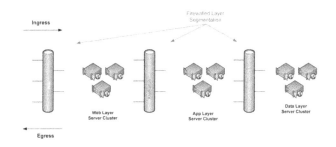

How do we leverage the benefits of a constantly growing ITTS that is changing rapidly without **Exponential Technological Advancements (ETA)** of its many different components?

To truly benefit from the improvements in technology, we have to leverage the power and improvements of a constantly growing ITTS. **Performance Engineering (PE)** is one of the technical catalysts that will leverage the advancements of a constantly growing ITTS. However, there is a procedural managerial process which can sit on top of any PE methodology or stand alone. This process starts with a top-down approach—meaning the process starts with the

Hierarchical Dissemination and Control of Information (HDCI).

Ultimately, we want to create a smarter enterprise organization. The key to making organizations smarter, whether they are government or commercial, is to apply the process of **Managing Smart Technology (MST)**. Technological advancements occur with more and more frequency. It is important that organizations understand that management techniques have to evolve and be agile enough to propagate the success of an organization or enterprise. To further support this fact, when we look back over the past twenty or more years, the same problems are in existence today. The technology has evolved, but the management practices of the technology remains the same.

The question we need to ask is: "Why do we still have the same problems when we have faster computers and more sophisticated software?" The answer to this question is this: "As technology has advanced over the course of years, it is time now for the management practices to evolve. The technology is smarter and

3

management should now make the adjustment to manage smart technology.

MST is the systematic top-down approach as to how an organization intelligently controls or leads its **Information Technology Component Systems (ITCS)** to strategically and operationally design and develop products and services to accomplish its desired goals and objectives, efficiently and effectively.

The MST process does not manage projects; it manages the technology. Projects often encounter a multitude of problems and delays because the technology is not being managed. When a project is being managed, the activities of managing the people and managing the technology should be in tandem. The management of the project and people is the norm, but the management of the technology is what has been missing.

It is highly imperative that the technology is managed to fully benefit from the improvements in the technology and to promote the success of **Information Technology Objectives (ITO)**.

ITOs are the factors that initiate the business or business needs of an ITCS. An ITCS is the overall organizational depiction of an enterprise's **Functional Information Technology System (FITS).** Most ITCSs can be broken down into multiple levels of granularity that identify independent FITSs. The individual FITSs can all share an ITO or they can have independent ITOs.

The concept of MST supports all different management and software development paradigms. Agile and waterfall methods can both benefit from MST because of its ability to support iterative and sequential process-driven methods.

MST is very agile and cost effective and promotes organizational growth. MST is key when applying concepts of Big Data because of the specificity and intricate understanding of the systematic effect of distributing large data sets across multiple systems. MST facilitates optimality of resources to achieve economies of scales. MST is a proponent of reusability and leveraging the benefits of Cloud computing to support an organization's ability to save money and efficiently increase its ability to grow and migrate to new technology, minimizing the cost of training and hardware and software procurement.

Many organizations have similar **Information Technology (IT)** infrastructures, but yet they have separate enterprise architectures. The process of MST supports the commonality between organizations and their governance and recommends the implementation of a **Unified Enterprise Architecture (UEA)** to support their business needs and goals. This activity is easily gained by utilizing the Cloud computing paradigm. Unified Enterprise Architecture is a uniformed shared approach for multiple organizations to strategically apply well defined comprehensive techniques to align a organizations Information Technology Component Systems with the overall business vision of the organization.

Once an organization utilizes the concepts of MST, it becomes smarter and positions itself to fully understand how to apply and implement new advances in technology into its ITTS. MST supports the advancements in technology,

and **Artificial Intelligence (AI)** is the wave of the now and tomorrow. Organizations need to understand how to apply current and new AI initiatives into their structure. Smarter organizations can identify how to benefit from AI and all of its advancements. Natural language processing is big and can satisfy some of the needs of an organization if applied properly. There are many components to AI, and as organizations get smarter, they can identify how to create AI components to satisfy their own needs. Cognitive processing is wide open, and it will truly impact smarter technological advancements. Understanding and applying the concept of **Machine Learning (ML)** will truly benefit many data-driven organizations and others. ML is the backbone of creating true cognitive computing systems and Research and Development (R&D) down this path can lead to building the most intelligent hardware and software systems possible.

Technical Organizational Alignment

Many organizations miss the mark on their ITOs for different reasons, but the key to successfully achieving ITOs is MST. The underlying concept of MST is to hierarchically manage **Information Technology (IT)** assets. Once again, this is done by the HDCI.

Figure B. Original Organization Chart

The management of IT assets can be done efficiently by applying the principal of **Technical Organizational Alignment (TOA).** This principal is supported by the participation of **Technical Resource Experts (TREs)**. The TREs are senior technical architects with acceptable **Discipline Defined Expertise (DDE)** in a subject matter. TREs are very important because they have the knowledge to ensure all activities related to an

ITO are moving in a positive manner. They also have the ability to identify problems which could stop or impede the success of the ITO, and they can identify solutions that will promote the success of the ITO. The activities can be anything from conducting meetings to creating the design of application software. It is important that all activities are conducted with a **Defined Goal and Purpose (DGP).**

When organizations are technically aligned, they have strategically placed specific technical architects in key positions throughout their hierarchy. The highest-level architect placement is normally at the L2 level in the hierarchy. This architect will work with all sublevel L2.1 architects to ensure that all ITOs are disseminated clearly and concisely as they are propagated down and technically managed to ensure success. The lowest-level architects work with the **Subject Matter Experts (SMEs)** to ensure that ITOs are being met technically by the SMEs and mitigate any technical issues relating to ITOs. Once ITOs are technically met, the results will be propagated upward.

Figure C. Organization Chart after Technical Organizational Alignment

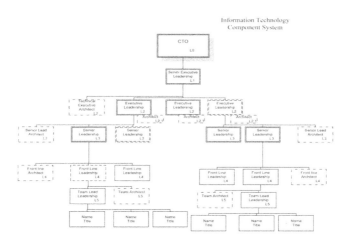

The **Principal of Technical Organizational Alignment (PTOA)** will help all levels of an organization succeed at achieving its ITOs. In most cases, the ITOs are the same, but different organizations must perform different task to ensure that the ITOs are successfully achieved.

Once the PTOA is applied, the organization is in position to successfully manage its IT assets. Successfully managing IT assets is achievable by applying **Accountability Rules (AR)** to every tier of an ITCS. There are two rules of

accountability that can be applied, **Two Phase Accountability (TPA)** and **Collaborative Tiered Accountability (CTA)**.

TPA takes place when the Technical Subject Matter Architect and the SME take responsibility for completing the low level technical task which yields the desired ITOs.

CTA takes place when the Technical Subject Matter Architect and his tiered manager along with the architect of the level above manage the success of the SME, ensuring all ITOs are met and all issues are mitigated.

The accountability rules are there to support the overall success of an organization. Once the accountability rules have been applied, all architects can **Level Set Objectives (LSO)** with their rules counterpart to ensure that all ITOs are being met.

The objective is to promote accountability throughout the various levels of an organization's hierarchy and across all FITSs that are affected by the Information Technology Objective. This

will allow upper management to focus on the organizations Functional Information Technical Systems and not on the technical aspects of the ITOs because the management's assets are protected by Technical Organization Alignment. This will allow management to report up the chain of command without having to be intricately involved with the technical work that is being done at the lower level of the hierarchy.

The PTOA is very important because it positions all leadership in the hierarchy for success. It will give leadership the ability to comfortably manage the efforts of the ITO from a high level without having to get to low level with all of the technical details. This will allow management to perform their managerial task and ensure that all other functions of the organization are being met.

MST and HDCI

An organization that is responsible for application development will typically follow some type of software development methodology. This methodology will be the driving force as to how the development is done from creation to implementation. MST will support any methodology followed by an organization because MST is independent of any chosen methodology. MST will ensure that the entire organization will be successful with achieving its ITOs.

An ITCS at the highest level initiates an HDCI. This information is typically in the form of an ITO. This ITO addresses a business need of the ITCS. The ITO is then pushed down to the FITS to perform work on the ITO to bring it to a state of completion. Each FITS applies a chosen method or methodology to initiate the work that has to be done to design, develop, and implement the ITO.

MST will allow an ITCS the ability to manage the ITO effectively and concisely, yielding cost-saving results. The ITO will be managed to a point of success without utilizing unnecessary resources to accomplish the task by applying the PTOA to ensure that the ITOs are technically managed to identify and mitigate risks.. This will yield successful implementation and execution of the ITOs.

Disciplined Defined Expertise

Technical Organizational Alignment Rating

Before TOA is done, an organization should obtain a **Technical Organizational Alignment Rating (TOAR)**. This rating will display the strength of the organization as it pertains to its ability to MST.

The TOAR is a score that is given to an organization based on the assessment of its TOA at each level of its hierarchy. There is an overall score and a score that is given for each level of the hierarchy that is assessed. The numbers range from 0 to 5; lowest rating being 0 and the highest being 5.

TOAR scoring is based on the alignment of the architects in the hierarchy and the **Discipline Defined Expertise (DDE)** of architects. This score is driven by the strength and skill set of the architects that are or are not in key positions within an organization's hierarchy.

Discipline Defined Expertise

Software Development Architect (SDA) – Individual who identifies performance solutions as well as development solutions for software development organizations. These architects ensure that technical and coding standards are being followed to obtain high levels of efficient consistency. The SDA should have at a minimum the following skills:

- Relational Database Management System (RDBMS)
- Operating system
- Programming languages
- Principal of multi-coalescent configuration
- Network knowledge
- Software performance engineer

Enterprise Architect (EA) – Individual who works with senior leadership and other SMEs to ensure that an organizations ITOs align with the business needs of the organization. Also, the enterprise architect must work across organizational boundaries to help facilitate that all FITSs are working together to ensure all organizational and business objectives are being met at every level within an organization. The EA should be familiar with the following skills:

- Understand management at the executive level
- Strong knowledge of enterprise architecture
- Principal of multi-coalescent configuration
- Up-to-date with latest technology trends
- Have the ability to explain complex technical issues
- Collaborative skills and project management
- Ability to understand how individual components interact with the whole system
- RDBMS

- Operating system
- Programming language
- Network knowledge
- Software performance engineer

Database Architect (DA) – Individual who should have the ability to design and create database applications and support development groups to satisfy data requirements for application needs. The database architect creates interfaces, data transfer mechanisms, and creates efficient access to data structures. The database architect should also have the ability to build tables for normalization and de-normalization as well data warehousing strategy. The DA should have the following skills:

- Strong knowledge of database performance tuning
- Design databases to support business applications, ensuring system scalability, security, performance, and reliability
- Develop data models for applications, metadata tables, views, or related database structures

- Principal of multi-coalescent configuration
- Develop load-balancing processes to eliminate down time for backup processes
- Develop or maintain archived procedures, procedural codes, or queries for applications
- Develop and document database architectures
- Develop database architectural strategies at the modeling, design, and implementation stages to address business or industry requirements
- Collaborate with system architects, software architects, design analysts, and others to understand business or industry requirements
- Create and enforce database development standards
- Demonstrate database technical functionality, such as performance, security, and reliability

Network Architect (NA) - Individual to design computer networks based on user and application needs. Must be able to execute multiple functions as they pertain to networks and telecommunications. The Network Architect should have an understanding as to how applications work as it pertains to network communication. The architect should have the ability to understand new technology trends to ensure that data networking trends are continuously improving. The NA should have the following skills:

- Understanding enterprise network design including WAN and LAN topologies and security concerns regarding DMZ implementation
- Network troubleshooting experience, which includes packet trace and Sniffer analysis, as well as switch configuration analysis
- Understanding and familiarity with firewalls and firewall configuration; understanding and familiarity with IPS devices and policy implementation
- Determines methods and procedures to be implemented and used on the most complex new technologies

- Experience with design, configuration, and support of reverse proxies to enhance performance
- Knowledge of data security
- Knowledge of intrusion detection systems
- Strong knowledge of enterprise network communications and connectivity
- Maintain computer hardware and network security
- Security experience as it applies to compliance, protection of assets, and company security

Systems Architect (SA) - Individual must have extensive knowledge of computer operating systems as well as a working knowledge of how applications behave on a system. Also, the Systems Architect should have strong knowledge of hardware and how to upgrade software and hardware. The SA should have the following skills:

- Have strong problem-solving skills
- Ability to troubleshoot hardware and software related issues

- Strong knowledge of Web technologies
- Strong knowledge of computer security
- Principal of multi-coalescent configuration
- Understanding of new computer security software and techniques
- Strong knowledge of system performance tuning
- Knowledge of database administration as it pertains to operating system
- Knowledge of network services that run on system and network administration
- Strong knowledge of application server setup and database server setup

Test Architect (TA) - Individual must have extensive knowledge of the software testing processing from beginning to end. This architect should have a strong knowledge of the ITTS; this will help test organization to understand how changes will impact the testing environment technically. The TA should have the following skills:

- Test environment knowledge
- Operating systems

- Programming
- Strong troubleshooting skills
- Hardware knowledge
- Test planning
- Test cases
- Test script
- Test data
- Test development
- Test execution
- Create test metrics
- Defect reporting
- Regression testing
- End-to-end testing

Technology Employee Administrative Mentality (TEAM)

The IT arena has many different SMEs such as: Enterprise Architects, Database Administrators (DBA), Systems Administrators (SA), Network Engineers, Software Engineers, Analysts, Testers, etc. The various SMEs have a work mentality that sometimes differs from each other. For example, software engineers may think differently than a DBA when it comes to working with others outside of their subject matter.

There are multiple ways to manage the IT staff, but the focus of this point will be based on a management technique that is geared towards the work mentality of the SME. We refer to this technique as **Technology Employee**

Administrative Mentality (TEAM). The meaning of TEAM is simply, the technical mentality and behavior of individual employees from different disciplines within the technology field.

People in the IT field often work in silos. Generally speaking, since IT staffers only concern themselves with the piece of work they are working on, they are somewhat technical introverts. Then there are others who think they are smarter than everyone because of the nature of their job. Also, you have those who think that they are devalued because of their job function and feel as if they must over emphasize the importance of their job. It is important that when managing different types of SMEs, one takes into consideration that the psyche of the SMEs can differ and understand why this is.

TEAM is a concept and approach that can help management get the best performance from their SMEs to support the overall function of the business. This concept can be very instrumental in building strong, successful teams.

Managing Smart Technology Performance Engineering

Strong knowledge of software development; database administration; Big Data; performance tuning; and system administration on Unix, Linux, and Windows platforms is very important when designing and building an optimal ITCS. Knowledge and understanding of software as it relates to the Operating Systems (OS) and its communication with DBMS (Oracle, Greenplum, Teradata) are vital and instrumental in quickly writing and retrieving information. **Performance Engineering (PE)** is a part of building and maintaining all components of an ITCS. This is the reason the MST concept plays such a pivotal role. The **Managing Smart Technology Performance Engineering**

(MSTPE) components can be applied to all phases of the software development life cycle.

The IT industry has grown tremendously over the past twenty years. Technology has gotten smarter. The evolution of hardware and software has been the key mechanism to its growth. The hardware has increased the IT industry's ability to process high volumes of data. The software has improved to a point in which software development can fully utilize the benefits of the hardware enhancements.

Despite the development of smarter technology, systems are still facing the same problems encountered twenty years ago. It's true that that a large amount of data can be manipulated and systems are now more robust. But they face the same problems: speed and time. The larger the system, the more the issues of speed and time come into play. Technology can continue to grow, but if businesses continue to use the same IT approach that they have been using for the past twenty years, then the old problems will always exist. Therefore, it is imperative that businesses implement the process of MSTPE.

The common approach that is being used by most businesses in IT is to use a particular software development methodology and apply it to the businesses' need. In doing this, businesses will use the latest and greatest technology and build a system that depends on linear scalability, never maximizing the full capability of the technology. In today's world and even yesterday's, this is not efficient utilization of technical resources. Speed and time are always the issue at some point. MSTPE will support full utilization of technical resources.

The silicon CPU chips being used now are maxed when it comes to speed. This means that, given the current technology, CPUs are running as fast as they can until the next evolution of processors. The speed of light is the next hurdle.

Even with the evolution of the computer chip and increased speed, the speed and time problem will continue to exist. We should now change our business approach to IT. We have to maximize the power of the current and new technology by applying the principal of MSTPE. This approach can be applied to all phases of the software development life cycle. This method is very agile and can be used iteratively or sequentially. The breakdown for the IT model is listed below:

1) Analysis - Perform an assessment of the business need. Identify **Key Performance Components (KPCs)** and then identify a **Performance Solution (PS)** to satisfy and achieve the specified business need.

2) Design - Create a design that will support the software and hardware KPCs.

3) Construction - Create software utilizing **Efficient Consistency (EC)** that will support the PS and construct and architect a hardware environment which will enable the software to perform optimally in an ITTS.

4) Testing - The software and the hardware configuration will be tested for a **High Level of Satisfaction (HLOS).**

5) Implementation (Production) - The desired/designed result will be implemented.

Key Performance Components

KPCs are defined as areas within the system that could significantly affect performance (i.e., platform, multi-tiered applications, connectivity etc.).

Performance Solution

The PS will be identified as the desired hardware configuration and development solution.

- Hardware Configuration – Cloud computing, high performance computing, GRID computing, distributed computing, etc.

  - Symmetric Multi-Processor(SMP) (Shared everything)
  - Massively Parallel Processor (MPP) (Shared nothing)
  - CLUSTER
  - VIRTUALIZATION

- Development Solution - Parallel programming, software architecture, etc.

  - Web
  - Process virtualization
  - Middleware
  - On-line Transaction
    Processing (OLTP)
  - On-line Analytical Processing (OLAP)
  - Content Management System (CMS)
  - Message queues
  - Relational Database Management
    System (RDBMS)
  - Big Data
  - In Memory Database System (IMDS)
  - Remote Procedure Call (RPC)

Efficient Consistency

EC is utilizing defined standards when devel-
oping software. This will yield a uniformed
development approach across all areas.

High Level of Satisfaction

HLOS is the acceptable response time from the hardware and software application from beginning to end.

The MSTPE approach to enhancing the performance of software systems can be applied to a system in its initial design to a system that currently exists. It is a methodical process. If an existing system needs to be improved from a performance perspective, we should do the following:

- Perform the upfront analysis, including understanding the functionality of the overall software system.
- Once this understanding is done then, observe how the application performs in an actual run time environment from beginning to end.
- Then, examine the behavior of the application to identify the largest bottleneck(s) in the system.
- Make the necessary changes to reconcile the identified problem.

It is important to perform final end-to-end tests, comparing the response times to the initial response times. A substantial improvement **will be** noticed. There are many factors and steps that have to be performed, that are mentioned later in this document, which will help to improve the performance of software systems in their current or existing state.

PE: Identify and reconcile problematic areas which may hinder the performance of a software application causing slow response time from the actual software application to slow response time due to poor hardware performance.

Scope: To identify a methodical approach to improving the performance of a software application or a hardware application server. Ultimately providing optimal scalability and throughput without compromising system integrity.

PE Methodology: Approach as to how to perform PE. It is an approach that has been developed from knowledge of software development, software architecture design, systems integration, database administration, systems administration, and understanding of MST concepts. This method of PE is derived from the state of the software system and the **Consolidation Approach (CA)** of software systems. The CA is the method that is used to identify how multiple applications running on a single hardware platform are combined. There are three different states of a software project: the **Initial State (IS)**, the **Transitional State (TS),** and the **Existing State (ES)**.

IS: The initial or beginning phase of the software development life cycle.

TS: The phase of the software development life cycle in which a design and even some source code has been defined. But, the system itself has not been fully completed.

ES: The phase in which an application has been implemented and is in a production or production-like environment.

CA: Multiple applications running on a single hardware platform, consolidated in a way which allows a server to be fully utilized and perform optimally.

INITIAL STATE

The concept of software performance is very important. Many projects choose to not deal with this concept until long after the application has been written and is running in a production environment. The mindset is generally that it is too time consuming to deal with the performance initially and, therefore, not cost effective. However, the cost that is encountered to improve the performance of software once it has been implemented and running in a production environment can be very costly as opposed to designing performance into the system and application.

The IS of an application is where performance can be addressed. If done properly, an application can be created in its inception with an optimal performance design. There are a number of things that can be considered when one performs the initial analysis and design of a software system. It is very important to have a good architect asking the right questions from all experts of a specified discipline that makes up a software system. This will get a project off in the right direction. The questions mentioned below are just some of the questions that should be asked when initially creating a software product. The questions may seem elementary or obvious but are actually often overlooked and forgotten until the software application is designed and is having performance issues.

In the IS, it is important to consider the following:

1. What type of platform will the application run on?
2. What are my business needs?
3. Is it a Web-based application, etc.?
4. Will the application be client server (two-tier or three-tier architecture)?
5. What type of front end (User Interface, etc.)?
6. What type of connectivity (Internet, etc.)?
7. What type of DBMS? There are also several factors that should be

considered when creating a software product during the IS such as:

FACTORS:

a. The use of threads (one-to-one, many-to-many)
b. The use of sockets
c. Synchronous/asynchronous request
d. Web services
e. Couple vs. decouple
f. Dynamic vs. static SQL
g. Middleware
h. Cohesion
i. Spatial locality
j. Temporal locality
k. Caching, paging
l. Shared memory
m. Message queues
n. Semaphores
o. Pipes
p. Transaction management

The aforementioned factors will all have an effect upon an applications performance. In the inception of an application, it would be very beneficial for a development organization to consider these factors when architecting a software application. Some of these factors, in conjunction with others, will yield an application that performs optimally if coded properly. On the other hand, if some of these factors are combined improperly, optimal performance will be hindered, because of resource allocation with competing processes.

During the logical or schematic design phase, performance can be addressed at a high level. Before the detailed design is done, the logical design can include the concepts of middleware, structured and unstructured database systems and programming approaches (procedural or objectivity).

During the technical or physical design, the usage of static SQL and dynamic SQL can be determined. Scalability can also be addressed during the technical design. Looking at the system requirements will help to gauge which type of technology would be best to satisfy the business needs of an ITCS. The physical design will allow for performance gains by taking advantage of individual nuisances that can sometimes be specific to various products (indexing, load balancing, data dependent routing, memory, etc.).

Once a good technical design has been completed, the actual writing of code can begin. To get optimal performance from the software, there should be a standard approach as to how resource allocation should be accomplished as well as defining best practices for various coding techniques to help facilitate a uniformed development effort. EC is key when writing or coding a good performing application.

TRANSITIONAL STATE

The TS of an application is a phase in which performance gains can be added. Of course, the concept of software performance is very important. Many projects choose not to deal with this concept until long after the application has been written and is running in a production environment.

The TS of an application is where performance can also be addressed. A system that is in the TS will either have an incomplete design or a complete design and possibly even has some written source code, but the system has not been fully coded. The stage of the TS will dictate where performance issues will initially be addressed. If the design has not been completed, then the work that has been done can be analyzed for inefficiencies. If any inefficiencies are found, they can be corrected. If the design has been completed then the logical and the technical design will be analyzed for inefficiencies and a performance assessment will be made, and the work will continue to the construction or coding stage of the life cycle.

EXISTING STATE

A software system that has been fully implemented and deployed is a system that is in the ES. Performance gains can be made in the ES, however, it is recommended to consider performance in the IS or the TS of a project if possible. Many software projects that have invested millions in a rewrite or redesign that are in the ES are no longer looking to do another rewrite or redesign. Projects that are in the ES can make performance enhancements in a couple of different areas. The hardware server that supports the software application can be tuned to yield performance gains. The software application itself can be modified to improve performance. The backend processing (database) can be adjusted to enhance performance. There are a number of factors which can be considered in improving a software system in the ES.

CONSOLIDATION APPROACH

The concept of PE is very important when grouping or consolidating different software applications on the same host server. A lot of software organizations try to fully utilize their hardware by piling as many applications on the hardware as they can. And when there seems to be a performance problem, the organization often times will purchase larger computers with a large amount of processing power to resolve the performance issue. Eventually, the bigger machines will experience the same performance problems as the smaller machines. This can be very costly. The CA to performance engineering is a method that is used to identify how multiple applications running on a single hardware platform can be combined in a way which will allow a server to be fully utilized and perform optimally. There are a number of factors to should be considered when combining software applications on the same host.

The MST approach to enhancing the performance of an ITTS in the ES is a methodically implemented process. Initially, upfront analysis of a system must be performed. This analysis includes gaining a high-level understanding of the functionality of the overall software system. Then perform an observation for **Initial Systemic Behavioral Metrics (ISBM)** based on how the application performs in the actual run time environment from beginning to end, baselining the initial response time of the system. Next is to examine the actual behavior of the application during run time, identifying the largest bottleneck in the system. Once the bottleneck has been identified, analyze the bottleneck and make the necessary changes to reconcile the

Identified Point of Contention (IPOC). The performance of the system should be tested once again by breaking down its component structure into smaller **Points of Measurements (POMs)** identifying other IPOCs.

Once all IPOCs have been reconciled, a final end-to-end test should be completed and the resulting response times should be compared to the ISBM. A substantial improvement will be noticed. The ultimate objective for projects in the ES is to improve or increase the scalability of the software system. The factors mentioned earlier in the ES introduction are just some of the enhancements that can be made to improve the performance of a software system in the ES. It is important to understand that an improvement to one component can have an undesired effect upon another component within the system. All improvements and changes must be a resultant of **Multi-Coalescent Configuration (MCC).** Therefore, it is highly imperative that all IPOC reconciliations are calculated, well thought out, and thoroughly tested.

IPOC - Determined area of resource bottleneck.

POM - Granular breakdown of software functional system components.

Optimal Behavior Factors (OBF) - The performance measurement of a software systems behavior.

OBF1 – The highest level of performance behavior of a software system

OBF2 – A high level of performance behavior for a software system with very little IPOC's

OBF3 – A medium or average behavior for a software system

OBF4 – A low-level behavior for a software system that functions but has multiple IPOC's

OBF5 – The lowest level of behavior for a software system

Multi Coalescent Configuration (MCC) – The systematic approach to configuring multiple hardware and software components to function with uniformity and optimality within a software environment.

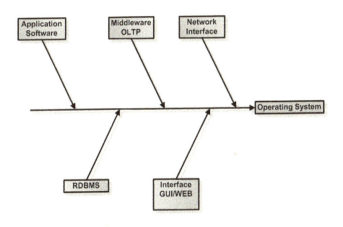

Figure 1.1 MCC

In MCC, all software components must communicate with the OS at some point in the paradigm. Each component can be configured to optimally communicate with the OS.

The common link between all software components is the OS. Software, whether it be application or commercial off-the-shelf (COTS) communicates with the OS. The OS is the key to software resource utilization (locality of reference, shared memory, stack, and heap). When software is configured, it is important to ensure that all OS resources used are set to an optimal level of usage for software utilization.

Many applications use some type of upper-level memory. This memory is there to be used, but there are always competing processes that utilize upper-memory as well. MCC is key to establishing a software environment with OBFs.

In order to truly design or improve an application system, MCC of the ITCS has to be done. The interaction of the OS, hardware and software has to be considered to properly design for optimal behavior or to improve performance of existing system. This sounds pretty straight forward in theory, but in order to achieve the best results it is highly imperative to understand what the abstraction layer between the OS, hardware, and the application is doing. This will allow for optimal usage of the system resources, hardware, and application.

Glossary

Accountability Rules (AR) rules that are applied on every tier of an Information Technology Component System (ITCS) to aid in the success of achieving its ITOs.

Collaborative Tiered Accountability (CTA) takes place when the Technical Subject Matter Architect and his tiered manager along with the architect of the level above manage the success of the SME, ensuring all ITOs are met and all issues are mitigated.

Level Set Objectives (LSO) is when management and all other parties come together to discuss the status of the ITOs and determine if objectives are being met and, if not, define a mitigation strategy.

Hierarchical Dissemination and Control of Information (HDCI) is the distribution from the top down of the overall information technology goals and objectives for a business or enterprise.

Information Technology Component System (ITCS) is the overall organizational depiction of an enterprises Functional Information Technology System (FITS).

Functional Information Technology System (FITS) is the specific functional goal of a business unit within an organization.

Information Technology Technical System (ITTS) – The hardware and software infrastructure components that make up a technical computer system environment.

Managing Smart Technology (MST) – The systematic top-down approach as to how an organization intelligently control or leads its ITCS to strategically and operationally design and develop products and services to accomplish its desired goals and objectives efficiently and effectively.

Technical Organizational Alignment (TOA)- *Placing key technical expertise at every level of the hierarchy.*

Technical Organizational Alignment Rating (TOAR) – *This is a score given to an organization based on the assessment of its TOA at each level of its hierarchy. There is an overall score and a score that is given for each level of the hierarchy that is assessed. The numbers range from 0 to 5; lowest rating being 0 and the highest being 5.*

Technical Resource Expert (TRE) – *Senior technical architects with acceptable discipline defined expertise in area of subject matter.*

Technology Employee Administrative Mentality – *The technical mentality and behavior of an individual employee from different disciplines within the technology field*

Two-Phase Accountability (TPA) - *takes place when the Technical Subject Matter Architect and the Subject Matter Expert take responsibility* *for completing the low-level technical task that yields the desired ITOs.*

***Unified Enterprise Architecture (UEA)** - is a uniformed shared approach for multiple orga-nizations to strategically apply well defined comprehensive techniques to align a organi-zations Information Technology Component Systems with the overall business vision of the organization.*